AIKIDO
A BEGINNER'S GUIDE TO TRADITIONAL AIKIDO

BY
MATS ALEXANDERSSON

AIKIDO A BEGINNER'S GUIDE TO TRADITIONAL AIKIDO

Copyright © 2016 Mats Alexandersson
ISBN-13: 978-1535599986
ISBN-10: 1535599987

Technique photos by Svante Larsson
Additional photos by Mats Alexandersson

Mats Alexandersson, 1965–
Aikido A Beginner's Guide To Traditional Aikido

Did you enjoy this book?
You may also find these books interesting.
You will find them on Amazon.

Aikido Osai Waza
Pinning Techniques In Traditional Aikido

In black/white
ISBN-10: 1530332974
ISBN-13: 978-1530332977

In full color
ISBN-10: 1499511418
ISBN-13: 978-1499511413

Aikido Nage Waza
Throwing Techniques in Traditional Aikido

In black/white
ISBN-10: 1530878810
ISBN-13: 978-1530878819

In full color
ISBN-13: 978-1530331307
ISBN-10: 1530331307

Aikido Buki Waza
Weapon techniques in Traditional Aikido

In black/white
ISBN-10: 1530757843
ISBN-13: 978-1530757848

In full color
ISBN-10: 1532752172
ISBN-13: 978-1532752179

CONTENTS

The idea of the beginner's guide 5

About aikido and training 5

Tai no henko 8
    Tai no henko Go tai 8
    Tai no henko Ju tai 10

Kokyu ho 12
    Morote dori kokyu ho 12
    Suwari waza kokyu ho basic form #1 14
    Suwari waza kokyu ho basic form #2 15

Ikkyo 16
    Ai hanmi katate dori ikkyo omote waza 17
    Ai hanmi katate dori ikkyo ura waza 18
    Gyaki hanmi katate dori ikkyo omote waza 20
    Gyaki hanmi katate dori ikkyo ura waza 22
    Shomen uchi ikkyo omote waza 24
    Shomen uchi ikkyo ura waza 26

Nikkyo 28
    Gyaki hanmi katate dori nikkyo omote waza 28
    Gyaki hanmi katate dori nikkyo ura waza 30
    Ai hanmi katate dori nikkyo ura waza 33
    Ryo kata dori nikkyo omote waza 36
    Ryo kata dori nikkyo ura waza 38

Kote gaeshi 40
    Ai hamni katate dori kote gaeshi 40

Shiho nage 46
    Gyaki hanmi katate dori shiho nage omote waza 46
    Gyaki hanmi katate dori shiho nage ura waza 48

Tenchi nage 50
    Ryote dori tenchi nage 50

Irimi nage 52
    Shomen uchi irmi nage 52

Kaiten nage 54
- Gyaki hanmi katate dori kaiten nage soto maware 54
- Gyaki hanmi katate dori kaiten nage uchi maware 56

Ai ki no Ken 60
- 1st suburi 60
- 2nd suburi 64
- 3rd suburi 68
- 4th suburi 74
- 5th suburi 79
- 6th suburi 86
- 7th suburi 90
- Shiho giri 94
- Happo giri 98

Ai ki no Jo 106
- Choku Tsuki 108
- Kaeshi Tsuki 109
- Ushiro Tsuki 110
- Tsuki Gedan Gaeshi 112
- Tsuki Jodan Gaeshi 114
- Shomen Uchi Komi 116
- Renzuko Uchi Komi 118
- Men Uchi Gedan Gaeshi 120
- Men Uchi Ushiro Tsuki 122
- Gyaku Yokomen Ushiro Tsuki 124

Wordlist for aikidokas 127

Some advice for students in a dojo 130

THE IDEA OF THE BEGINNER'S GUIDE

The idea behind these excerpts from the three books, Aikido Osai Waza, Aikido Nage Waza and Aikido Buki Waza, is to give a beginner student a short introduction to some of the basic techniques in traditional aikido also commonly refered to as Iwama aikido. During the first year a beginner should encounter a variety of basic techniques, empty handed as well as weapons techniques. This will give any beginner student an opportunity to start to understand the concept of Riai. The profound connections between tai jutsu and buki waza.

THOUGHTS ABOUT AIKIDO AND TRAINING

About training aikido as a martial art
Aikido is a true martial art with long historical references and heritage, not the least in Daito Ryu Aiki Jujutsu. Daito Ryu Aiki Jujutsu is the base of most of the techniques in aikido, then transformed into aikido by the founder Morihei Ueshiba, O-Sensei. Aikido is orginated from systematized close combat techniques and has all the makings for an efficient martial art and self defence. However the mere training of aikido techniques will not be sufficent. The attitude and seriousness in training is equally important. If you want to develop the right skills you need to train with this in mind and of course invest a lot of time energy over many years. There is no quick fix to learn and master traditional aikido or any true martial art. You may learn a lot of techniques quickly, but then again only in a more superficial way. Training over a length of time will help you to gain a deeper understanding of the techniques and importantly, the system of takemusu aikido.

Open vs closed skills in aikido
Most of the time in practice we work in the area of closed skills. Which means a set situation with specific circumstances and mind set of both nage and uke. This could for instance be a predefined practice of one technique with a certain form of attack. This is a very efficient method for learning since it often involves a pace set by nage and sometimes by nage and uke together. This gives time and opportunity to focus on the details as well as the whole aspect of the techniques. This is invariable the most common way to practice in aikido, since the demands on the technical level is very high. The only way to thoroughly learn and master the techniques is working with the closed skills. Most often known as kihon waza, basic forms and training.
Open skills in martial arts would be when the set situation is not set at all and when the pace of what will happen may not be set by nage but also by the environment, uke in this case. This means not having predefined what will happen, not the techniques nor the attacks. This will demand a very high level of flexibility and mastering of the technical curriculum/matrix of the aikido, of the basic forms, variations (henka waza), and applied forms (oyo waza) and even in the actual moment as the unkown situation occurs adapt to create new variations based on the foundation in aikido. Open skills in it's most pure form is what we would call take musu aiki. Naturally the practice is done with different degrees on the scale of open-closed skills. For instance you will practice with ki no nagare forms, then move on to randori with more or less set content and number of attackers.

Ukemi and receiving attacks

Ukemi is often thought of as taking fancy falls when being thrown. This is true to some extent however ukemi is more a tool for understanding the technique than showing off. Through ukemi you, as uke, get to understand the other side of the coin, what a technique should be like. As uke you also give your self as a tool for nage to perfect his technique. When training in a correct manner nage will be able to perform with full power and speed. It is naturally vital that uke delivers honest attacks with the full consciousness of a sincere attacker. In this sense nage and uke grow strong together and benefit from their mutual goal.

Multiple attackers/attacks

An important reflection on how to perform and think of aikido is the concept of multiple attackers/attacks. Even though in most circumstances aikido is practised in pairs. The manner of how you practise is heavily influenced by the the notion of having multiple attackers. This of course defines what concerns must be met in performing the techniques. Later on for any aikidoka, you will encounter randori practice. Randori is a practice where one person handles multiple attackers. When training and when executing the techniques in aikido, even when only in pairs, you therefore always keep in mind that there would be more than one attacker. This in itself should affect your stance, your movements and how you end the technique. In these circumstances, awase, movement and technical proficiency in the basic techniques requires a high standard. The way to get there is to invest considerable time and effort in the basic training. The higher level of mastery of the basics, the better base for advanced practice.

Atemi

Atemi is often defined as a distracting blow to the opponent. I would like to add that they also should be effective in the sense of actual attacks. O-Sensei and Saito Sensei often said that atemi is 99% of aikido, there by pointing out the utmost importance of atemi in aikido. In any real situation absence of atemi is more than a gamble and vouches for uncertain outcome of the situation. But there is also a tacit knowledge in using correct atemis. Many practitioners do not realize the correct distance to the opponent is relative to execute a correct atemi. If in the distance to being able to perform an atemi correctly, you also are in the correct distance having entered and or entering into the technique. A lot of times, atemi is delivered too far away to be effective and consequently the person is too far away to effectively perform the technique. The remedy is to study atemi and actually train atemi to fully understand how to execute atemi. Saito Sensei trained, previously to entering the dojo of O-Sensei, Kendo, Judo and Karate. There are many different martial arts where the technical curriculum is mainly based on strikes and kicks. It is an excellent additional training to your aikido to actually train any of these martial arts. This will not only enable you to execute multiple atemis in flowing forms but also give you understanding of basic attacks often used in aikido and other attacks you may want to understand as well.

Zanshin

Zanshin is the state of mind you train your self to enter and stay in. It is an effortless awareness of all things around. Zanshin is a relaxed and alert awareness. Often zanshin is also referred to the prolonged focus after having executed a technique to emphasize the importance of not letting go mentally and phsyically.

Awase

Blending in aikido is what you do at all times. The blending is highly intuitive and a skill perfected over time through consciously forging your mindset. Awase may manifest itself in pure technical terms as timing with a movement or the very presence in any given situation. At the surface you may seem reactive, however in aikido you always maintain the initiative even though it seemingly is a respons to an opponents movement. A good way for describing this is to talk in the terms of; Go No Sen - response to the attack/after the attack is manifested. You allow the opponent to attack in this sense and therefore are in full awase with your opponent, mentally as well as physically. You can further divide the critical moments in time with two more concepts; Sen no Sen - before the attack is manifestested, and Sensen no Sen - at the same time as the attack. At the surface they describe when the attack is met, but from the awareness point of view, you always are in tune and blending as soon as the situation emerges. All the basic forms in aikido start out with nage seizing the direct initiative, forcing uke to action.

Kiai

Kiai can be silent, kiai can be a loud shout with it's base in the abdomen used for tactics or the result of excerting a tremendous physical power in a technique. To excert a kiai you need the proper breathing as described in kokyu ho. Kiai may be very beneficial in practice to heighten your focus and awareness. Train with kiai so it will become a natural part of your aikido even though many younger in aikido at first may find it somewhat embarrassing. Needless to say, this is an essential part of aikido.

TAI NO HENKO - GO TAI

1. The starting position. Start one step apart from each other.

2. Nage initiates the technique by extending his hand towards uke and forces uke to react to his movement.

3. Uke grabs the wrist.

4. Nage maintains his hand in the center of his body. At the same time nage takes a step forward to the side of nages foot, toe to toe.

TAI NO HENKO - GO TAI

5   There is a saying that goes; the head leads the hands and the hip leads the feet. This means that nage first turns his head, then the hand. This is followed by the hip turn which in it self will force the feet to move.
Nage turns the hip a full 180 degree turn. Nage keeps his hand in his center all the way through the movement.
The movement is a spiral movement which begins at the top and spirals down to the bottom. Nage then momentarily midthrough the technique end up in another hanmi position.

6   After nage completes the 180 degree hip turn, nage then moves the foot into the final position. Nage makes sure to be in a strong and well balanced position.

7   Nage keeps the hands in the center of his body. The hands are kept at shoulder width and just above the hip. Note that the wrists are distinctively below the elbows. Nage should be strong in this position and not easily moved. Nages center and hands should be stable in the following directions; forward, backward and up- and downward. When nage enters the final stance, nage should have a low and stable feeling and lower his hip very much the same he would when he strikes with the bokken.

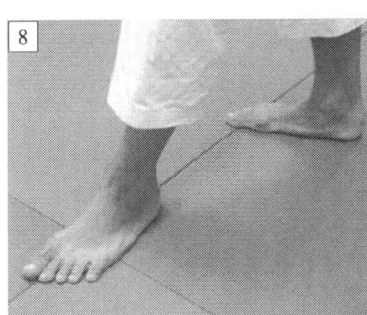

8   Hanmi is the recurring stance in practice. In this position you create a triangular stance refered to as hi-toemi. The idea behind it's design is to create a defensive and offensive stance. The stance is highly flexible and easily changes direction with a correct hip turn.

9   The proper stance is vital for body movement and correct hip movement. Your body rests on both feet with the weight equally distributed. The legs are slightly bent.

TAI NO HENKO - JU TAI

1. In the Ju Tai form nage and uke start out further apart than in the Ki hon form (the go tai form). The reason for this is that in the go tai form when you practise you are already in a position where contact is obtained. In the ki no nagare form, you start out in maai. The correct distance, in most situations is called, maai. Maai means harmonious distance. Maai is the relative distance between nage and uke where either of the two can not be reached unless one of them takes one step forward. The distance it self is not fixed, it depends on either persons length and build. In time and with practise you will learn how to intuitively estimate the distance.

2. Nage initiates the technique by stretching out the hand towards uke. Thus forcing uke to react to your movement. Both uke and nage move forward towards each other in order to close the distance between them. It is imperative for uke to react as soon as possible in order to make sure the movement from nage does not evolve in to a full blown attack.

3. Uke grabs the wrist with a strong grip in order to gain control of nage's hand.

4. As uke grabs the wrist nage blends and steps off the attacking line, toe to toe. Nage turns the head, hand, hip and feet in that order. The movement is a spiral movement going from the head down to the feet.

TAI NO HENKO - JU TAI

5   Nage continues the turn making sure coming off the line of attack.

6   Once the full 180 degree hip turn is completed, nage moves the foot into the final position.

MOROTE DORI KOKYO HO

Morote dori kokyo ho can simply be described as a motion where nage makes two 180 degree turns, while raising the arm up and then cutting down. Saito Sensei often explained and viusualized the movement using a bokken, raising the bokken while turning and cutting in the other direction. You will find it helpful having this image in mind while practising. It will help you to keep your center and focus in the technique. The benefits from practicing morote dori kokyo ho are several as with any kokyo ho practice.

Kokyo ho is one foundation in aikido that is always present.It involves focusing breathing with body movement and forging your mind into one with the above.

When nage executes the technique, nage inhales when moving in, and exhales when executing the second part of the technique, raising, turning and cutting down.

1   Uke grabs nage's arm with both hands.

2   Nage steps in, toe to heel, and lowers the elbow. Nage has a low feeling in shoulders and hip.

3   Nage turns the hip 180 degrees and maintains the same low position all the way through. When nage turns the hip, nage steps in and turns the hip deep in so that nage places himself side by side with uke's hip and shoulder.

4   Nage turns the hip and starts raising the arm in that movement with a feeling of executing shomen uchi.

MOROTE DORI KOKYO HO

5   Uke loses his balance. Nage then takes a step in closer to uke. Nage focuses the kokyu through tegetana all the way through.
A common mistake is to shift the focus to where contact may be made throughout the technique.

6   Nage continues the movement and cuts downwards. Nage ends the technique in a stable position, the hands are in line with the shoulders and in the same height as the hip. Nage is facing away from uke for several reasons. One reason is to visually control the environment. Since nage already has a clear understanding of where uke is, there is no need to look in that direction. Another reason is to protect the face, as when uke takes a high fall, the feet may come close.

7   This is the position when nage has turned the hip 180 degrees and stepped in close to uke. Shoulder to shoulder, and hip to hip in a low position. (Compare to picture no 3.)

SUWARI WAZA KOKYU HO BASIC FORM #1

1. Uke and nage start out in seiza. Uke grabs nage's both wrists at shoulder height and the hands are being held apart at shoulder width.

2. Nage turns the hip and simultaneously moves one knee forward diagonally. Nage cuts down across uke's wrist with one tegetana and with the other arm lowers the elbow to apply pressure from below. The pressure with from the hand goes through ukes grip, his arm and across his center. At the same time, nage slides to the side with one knee and the rest of the body follows as nage moves in shikko.

3. As uke falls to the side nage follows through and maintains the pressure with both hands.

4. Nage ends the technique sitting in seiza. Nage places one knee close by uke's armpit and the other close by the arm. Nage is maintaining a strong pressure on uke and uke maintains his focused grip.

SUWARI WAZA KOKYU HO BASIC FORM #2

1. Uke grabs nage's both wrists.

2. Nage extends his arms with the kokyo movement pressing upwards thereby forcing uke's elbows upwards.

3. Nage slides to the side with one knee. Nage maintains the pressure against uke and presses uke to the side.

4. Nage ends the technique sitting in seiza. Nage places one knee close by uke's armpit and the other close by the arm. The pressure is directed towards the center of uke and pins him down.

AI HANMI KATATE DORI IKKYO OMOTE WAZA

1. Nage stretches out the hand and uke grabs the wrist.

2. Nage drops slightly to enter from a low position.

3. Nage takes a step in front of uke and grabs the elbow from below. Nage's front foot is basically between uke's feet. The distance away from uke's body is as a rule of thumb, nage's shoulder width. Note the position of uke. Ideally you want uke's body to rest mainly on ukes back foot, which immobilizes uke. However nage does not push uke too far since this only leads nage to lose control of uke. Nage aims to not pass the center line of uke´s body.

4. By pushing the elbow from below, nage reveals the soft side of the wrist. This is where nage wants to grab. If nage grabs to soon, nage will end up with a grip where one hand pushes and the other pulls, thus making the technique less effective. Nage holds uke's arm pretty much as one would hold a bicycle handlebar.

AI HANMI KATATE DORI IKKYO OMOTE WAZA

5. Nage turns his hip and cuts down with his arms. This makes uke lose the balance and places uke with both feet, one knee and one hand on the mat. Nage maintains the pressure all the way through. It is vital that the next step only occurs after uke has completly lost balance. Nage steps in with the leg closest to uke. If nage steps in too soon there is a great risk that uke may counter that movement.

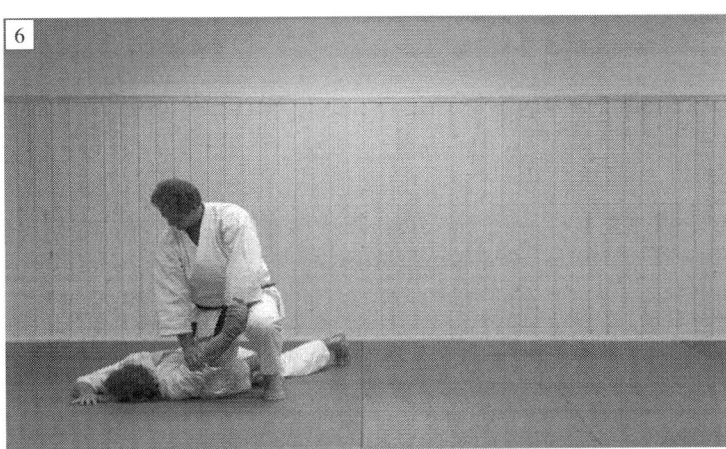

6. Nage put uke's shoulder to the mat. Nage then places his knee closest to uke just by the armpit and maintains the pressure. By securing the shoulder to the mat first, nage can more easily and safely continue with the pin.

7. Nage sits with both knees close to uke's armpit and wrist. Nage keeps his feet tightly together so the knees and feet form a triangle. Keeping the feet together will give nage a strong base and a balanced position.

8. Uke's arm should point 90 degrees out from the body. Uke's elbow should be flat on the mat with the back of the elbow joint facing upwards.
Nage should have one knee tightly by the armpit, the other by the wrist. As nage presses the elbow down, nage also applies a pressure that leads outwards away from uke's body.

AI HANMI KATATE DORI IKKYO URA WAZA

1. Nage stretches out the hand and uke grabs firmly.

2. Nage raises the hand in order to take a step in towards uke. Step 2 and 3 happens almost simultaneously. Basically the whole movement is a spiral movement going up and then down on the outside of uke.

3. Nage enters from below and takes a step toe to toe and applies pressure to nages elbow. Nage grabs the wrist at the same time. Nage avoids pushing uke's arm across ukes center line. Nage keeps his hands in his own center at all times.

4. Nage continues the movement, turns the hip and lowers the arms. When nage moves, nage does not move his feet until the turn of the hip forces the feet to actually move. The whole body movement orginates from the hip, starts from the head and leads down to the feet.

AI HANMI KATATE DORI IKKYO URA WAZA

5. Nage turns the hip until uke drops to the mat. Nage then takes the step sideaways so he will end up in a horse stance in a 90 degrees angle from the starting point. This is a stable and powerful position from where nage can continue.

6. Nage pushes uke's shoulder to the mat to secure the pin.

7. Nage sits with both knees close to uke's armpit and wrist. Nage keeps the feet tightly together so that the knees and feet form a triangle.

GYAKI HANMI KATATE DORI IKKYO OMOTE WAZA

1. Nage shows the hand and uke grabs strongly.

2. Nage slides 90 degrees sideways into horse stance and executes an atemi. Nage holds a strong feeling of kokyo in the arm being grabbed. The posture is low and stable.

3. Nage puts the hand on top of uke's hand grabbing the wrist. This is to secure the grip so that uke can not let go.

4. Nage turns the hip to enter from below. Nage uses kokyo power to extend the arm, grabs the elbow and pushes uke off balance.

GYAKI HANMI KATATE DORI IKKYO OMOTE WAZA

5 Nage continues the movement until uke lies on the mat.

6 Nage first secures the shoulder to mat and then executes the ikkyo pin.

7 Detail. Note the grab around uke's wrist. It is similiar to nikkyo, however the pin is still an ikkyo pin since the arm is being held 90 degrees out from uke's body and is pinned to the mat.

GYAKI HANMI KATATE DORI URA WAZA

1. Uke grabs the extended arm.

2. Nage slides sideways 90 degrees off the attacking line. Nage moves into a low position and executes an atemi.

3. Nage secures uke's grip on the wrist and prevents uke from letting go of the wrist.

4. Nage enters from below, maintains a low position and steps in toe to toe. When nage enters the body turn nage always keeps the arms in his center.

GYAKI HANMI KATATE DORI IKKYO URA WAZA

5 Nage continues the hip movement until reaching the horse stance position. Nage cuts down the arm in the center.

6 Nage continues the movement until uke drops to the mat.

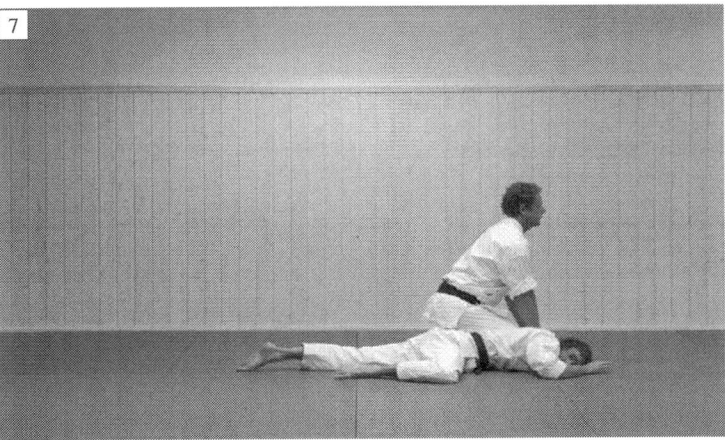

7 Nage ends the technique with the ikkyo pin.

SHOMEN UCHI IKKYO OMOTE WAZA

1. Nage initiates the technique in ai hanmi.

   Note on Shomen uchi
   All movements are initiated from the hip movement. Shomen uchi is a strike with the tegetana, the edge of the hand. The strike is vertical. The movement may work both as offense as defence. Nage raises the arm in nage's center which protects the center entering, then strikes straight down in the center.

2. Nage iniates the technique by raising the hand to enter into a strike. Uke mimics the movement with his hand. The hands connect in the movement while going upwards and the contact is smooth as if it is harmonized on it's path.

3. Nage takes a step in front of uke and simultaneously grabs the elbow.

4. Nage cuts down uke's arm. Only after this step, rendering uke completely off balance, it is possible for nage to take the next step.
   The most common mistake is to prematurely take the next step or even to skip this step. Doing so will create a very unstable posture, making nage vulnerable to a counter attack.

SHOMEN UCHI IKKYO OMOTE WAZA

5   When uke is completely off balance nage can take the next step. Nage steps in with the leg closest to uke and maintains the pressure the whole time.

This step is vital in all the omote forms of ikkyo, nikkyo, sankyo, yonkyo and rokkyo.

6   Nage ends the technique with the ikkyo pin.

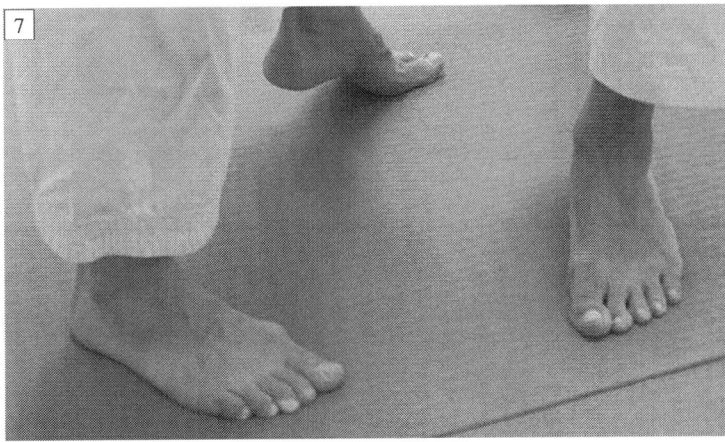

7   As seen in picture no. 3 nage takes ukes balance, and ideally uke will have the body weight on his back foot, rendering it difficult to move away.

SHOMEN UCHI IKKYO URA WAZA

1. Nage and uke start the technique in ai hanmi.

2. Nage initiates the technique with shomen uchi and uke mimics the movement. The hands gains contact on the upward movement.

3. Nage takes a step in toe to toe and drops into a low position. At the same time nage grabs the wrist and elbow, and applies pressure to uke.

4. Nage continues the movement by turning the hip and keeps the arms in his center. Nage pushes uke forward and off the attacking line in a spiral movement leading downwards.

SHOMEN UCHI IKKYO URA WAZA

5   As uke drops to the mat nage maintains a stance similar to horse stance.

6   Nage continues the movement into the ikkyo pin.

GYAKI HANMI KATATE DORI NIKKYO OMOTE WAZA

1. Uke grabs nage's wrist.

2. Nage slides 90 degrees of the attacking line into horse stance, strikes an atemi and stretches the arm in order to break uke's balance.

3. Nage grabs uke's wrist.

4. Nage takes a step forward in front of uke, simultaneously grabs the elbow from below and starts bringing uke down to the mat.

GYAKI HANMI KATATE DORI NIKKYO OMOTE WAZA

5   When uke has dropped to the mat, nage is ready to take a step with the leg closest to uke.

6   Nage then pins the shoulder to the mat and places the knee close to uke´s armpit.

7   Nage ends the technique with the nikkyo pin.

8   Detail pictures. Nage either grabs the lapel (a) or just cuts inwards with tegetana (b). Nage wants both shoulders to be firmly placed on the ground, along with uke's chest. Nage presses down one shoulder with the back of his hand just where the hand meets the wrist. This part of the hand is not flexibel and will give a firm support. Nage grabs uke's arm and pulls the arm tightly to the chest seeking to get as much contact as possible. The more contact nage gains the more power can be transfered trough uke's arm. Keeping uke's arm slightly bent will also give an oppurtunity to strengthen the physique around the shoulder.

GYAKI HANMI KATATE DORI NIKKYO URA WAZA

1 Uke grabs nage by the wrist.

2 Nage slides into horse stance, 90 degrees off the attacking line, strikes an atemi and stretches out the arm to further break uke's balance.

3 Nage grabs uke's wrist.

4 Nage takes a step in toe to toe, in a 45 degree angle off the attacking line. In the same movement, nage also lifts uke's wrist to the chest and pins it tightly. This movement makes sure uke's wrist will bent in a 90 degree angle.

GYAKI HANMI KATATE DORI NIKKYO URA WAZA

5. Nage turns hip and body towards uke and maintains the strong pressure on uke's wrist as well as uke's arm. This movement will make uke's arm bend at the elbow in 90 degrees.

6. Nage rolls uke's wrist around it's own centre, just by lowering the hip and advancing towards uke. Uke will then be forced to drop to the mat.

7. Nage places his tegetana from below on uke's elbow.

8. Nage cuts down the elbow and leads uke into nage's center. Nage pins uke's shoulder to the mat using the back of the hand. Nage also maintains the pressure on uke's wrist.

GYAKI HANMI KATATE DORI NIKKYO URA WAZA

9   Nage sits down and switches hands for the final stage of the pin. First the upper hand slides down to press against uke's shoulder.

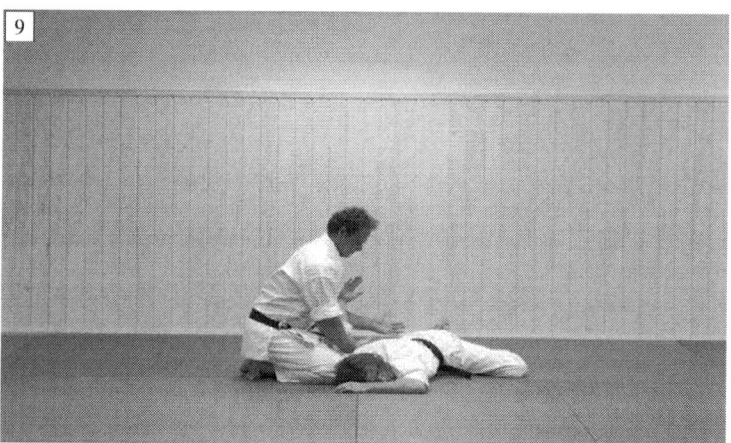

10 Then the other arm will scoop up uke's arm by the elbow and press the arm tightly to the chest.

11 Nage tightly pins uke to the mat. Nage finishes the pin and turns the hip and pushes uke's arm diagonally across uke's head.

AI HANMI KATATE DORI NIKKYO URA WAZA

1 Uke grabs nage's wrist.

2 Nage puts his hand on top of uke's grab in order to prevent uke to let go of the grip.

3 Nage raises the arms.

4 Nage takes at step in toe to toe and moves into an angel of 90 degrees off the attacking line. At the same time nage grabs around uke's wrist. Uke's wrist is also now in a 90 degree angle.

AI HANMI KATATE DORI NIKKYO URA WAZA

5   Nage turns the hip and by doing so forces uke to bend the arm into a 90 degree angle by the elbow.

6   Nage lowers the hip and cuts down with a rolling motion around uke's wrist. Note that nage not just simply presses down the hand. The movement is a circular movement around the center of uke's wrist.

7   Nage maintains the pressure against the wrist and at the same time nage grabs the elbow.

8   Nage then applies pressure and leads uke down in front of himself and secures the shoulder to the mat.

AI HANMI KATATE DORI NIKKYO URA WAZA

9. Nage puts one knee close the shoulder and head. Nage also applies pressure to the shoulder with the back of the hand.
Note, in this position, if nage would by accident drop the arm of uke, the arm will be caught by the leg next to the arm.

10. Nage shifts the positions of the hands. Nage tightly pins the arm to the chest and presses the shoulder firmly to the mat. The pressure of the arm against the chest should be very strong. The more contact, the better effect of the pin. Nage then turns the hip and presses the arm diagonally across uke's head and maintains the shoulder tightly pressed to the mat.

RYO KATA DORI NIKKYO OMOTE WAZA

1. Uke grabs both shoulders.

2. Nage slides 90 degrees off the attacking line into horse stance, strikes an atemi and extends the arm. The position is low and very stable.

3. Nage then grabs uke's hand and the elbow from below.

4. Nage takes a step in front of uke, at the same time pushes the elbow upwards.

RYO KATA DORI NIKKYO OMOTE WAZA

5 Nage continues the hip movement and cuts down nage's arm. With the same movement nage frees himself from the grip on the shoulder.

6 Nage ends the technique with the nikkyo pin.

RYO KATA DORI NIKKYO URA WAZA

1. Uke grabs both shoulders.

2. Nage slides off the attacking line into horse stance, 90 degrees of the attacking line. At the same time nage strikes an atemi and extends the arm.

3. Nage grabs uke's hand and also grabs the elbow from below.

4. Nage steps in toe to toe in an 45 degree angle. Nage turns the hip and with this movement nage ensures uke's wrist to bend in 90 degrees.

RYO KATA DORI NIKKYO URA WAZA

5. Nage continues the hip movement towards uke, bends the arm in 90 degrees and executes the nikkyo. Uke drops to the mat.

6. Nage switches grip and pushes with his tegetana on the elbow in order to lead uke down in front of nage's own center.

7. Nage secures the shoulder to the mat. Nage presses down the shoulder with the back of the hand.

8. Nage completes the technique with the nikkyo pin.

AI HANMI KATATE DORI KOTE GAESHI

1. Uke grabs nage's wrist.

2. Nage steps in toe to toe, turns the hip and moves 90 degrees off the attacking line. At the same time nage grabs uke's hand across the thumb and palm.

3. Nage enters into horse stance, breaks uke's balance and prepares to get out of uke's grip around the wrist.

4. Nage lowers the elbow and uses kokyo power to exit through the grip. Nage exits the grip between uke's thumb and index finger.

AI HANMI KATATE DORI KOTE GAESHI

5 Nage puts his palm on top of uke's hand. The fingers of both hands are parallel.

6 Uke's arm and wrist should now be in 90 degree angles. Uke prepares to turn the hip and simultaneously twist ukes hand in direction of the joint's natural direction.

7 Nage rolls uke's wrist so that uke falls down to the mat.

8 As uke falls, nage maintains the grip on uke's wrist.

AI HANMI KATATE DORI KOTE GAESHI - STANDING PIN

9   Nage pushes uke's hand to uke's face.

10 Nage shifts the grip with one hand and grabs uke's the elbow. Nage still maintains uke's hand in his own face.

11 Nage turns uke over to his stomach, pinning the shoulder tightly to the mat.

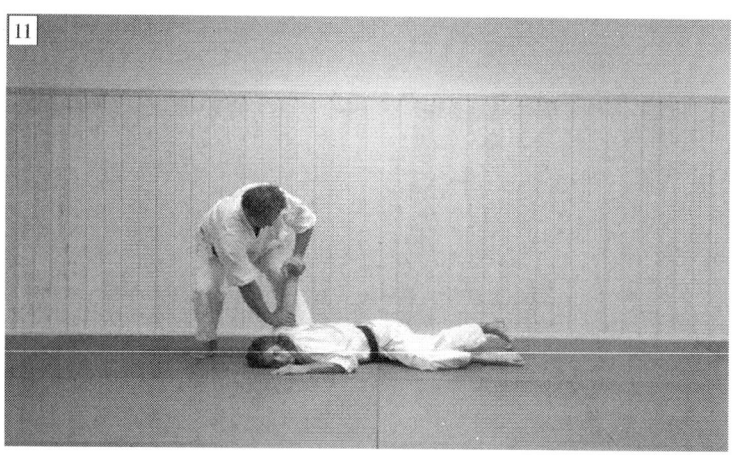

12 Nage grabs uke's wrist with both hands. Nage's hands are resting on top of the back of uke's hand. Note, if nage only grabs with one hand, there is a good chance uke may be able to free himself from the pin.

The inside of the old dojo in Iwama kept in a meticulous condition by the caretaker and dojo cho, Morihiro Saito Sensei, at the time of the picture.

AI HANMI KATATE DORI KOTE GAESHI - SITTING PIN

1. This is an alternate pin when sitting down.
   Nage pins uke's shoulder to the mat. One knee is placed by the head of uke.

2. Nage slides the hand from the shoulder to the wrist.

3. Nage grabs the wrist and pins the arm tight against his chest, and places the other knee by the shoulder.

4. Nage uses the arm to press uke's arm against the chest. Nage turns the hip and upper body diagonally across uke's head.

AI HANMI KATATE DORI KOTE GAESHI

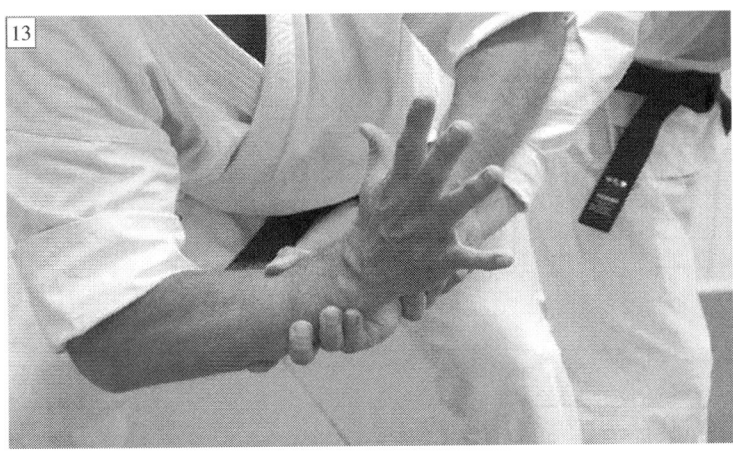

13 Detail. Extend your kokyo power trough the hand and fingers.

14 Lower the elbow and push the hand with kokyu through uke's grip. You will find the way between the thumb and index finger.

15 Nage puts his hand on top of uke's hand. The hand is placed so that the fingers are parallel. Ideally nage seeks for two 90 degree angles, one at the wrist and one by the elbow. Uke's forearm should be held horisontal.

16 Nage twists uke's wrist in the natural direction of the joint. By doing so there is no inherent resistance. The movement is, so to say, to roll the hand into a small ball.

GYAKI HANMI KATATE DORI SHIHO NAGE OMOTE WAZA

1. Uke grabs nage by the wrist.

2. Nage turns the hip, steps 90 degrees off the attacking line and simultaneously grabs uke's wrist. Nage grabs uke to secure the grip and prevent uke from escaping.

3. Nage steps in and raises the arm. Nage will keep the hands in front of the center of his head all the way through the upcoming turn.
It is most important that nage steps in and raises the arm at the same time. Otherwise nage risk his balance or not having enough strength to enter.
Common misstakes are for instance; Stepping in and raise the arms afterwards. Nage may not have the strenght to continue. Raising arm prior to stepping in. Nage may be pulled off balance.

4. Nage turns hip and body 270 degrees. At the very end nage releases the hand from uke's grip.

GYAKI HANMI KATATE DORI SHIHO NAGE OMOTE WAZA

5   Nage completes the full turn and ends up with uke's hand behind his own center. This makes uke's position weak and easy for nage to complete the throw.

6   Nage throws uke and ends the technique with the shiho nage pin.

7   Detail. When executing shiho nage, nage always grabs with his hands crossed. If nage grabs differently the hold will in itself block the movement.
Nage also presses uke's hand tightly against his own wrist to create as much contact as possible.

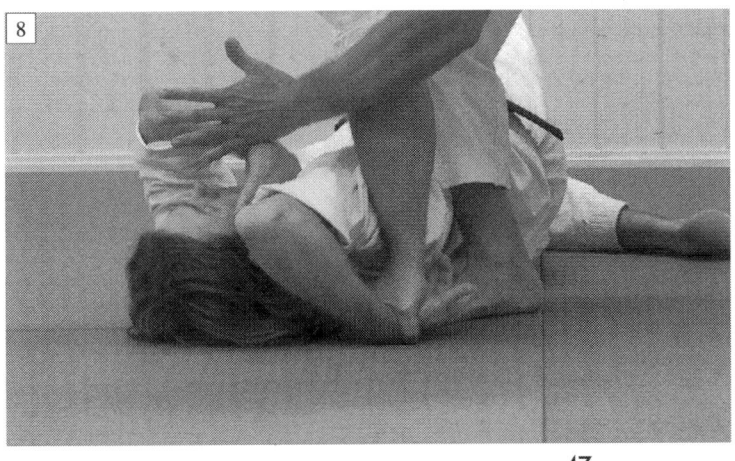

8   Detail. Nage grabs around the wrist in the same way as in yonkyo, pinning the wrist to the mat. There should be enough applied pressure so that uke's shoulder is stretched up and back which also helps pinning uke.
Nage stands approximately with a 45 degree angle to uke's torso with the leg closest to uke as the front leg. If uke would try to grab hold of uke and pull him down, this stance will prove to be the most stable.
Nage ends the technique by executing an atemi to uke's head.

GYAKI HANMI KATATE DORI SHIHO NAGE URA WAZA

1. Uke grabs nages wrist.

2. Nage grabs hold of uke's wrist, steps in toe to toe and drops low.

3. Nage turns hip and body and raises the arm. Nage will keep the hands in the center all the way through the hip turn.

4. Nage turns the body 180 degrees. At the very end of the turn when nage finally have to, nage takes a step in order to complete the turn.

GYAKI HANMI KATATE DORI SHIHO NAGE URA WAZA

5 Nage holds uke's arm and cuts down with the same feeling as striking with bokken.

6 Nage ends the throw with the pin.

7 Detail. Nage frees himself from the hold by twisting the arm with kokyu power out of uke's hand through the grip of the thumb.

RYOTEDORI TENCHI NAGE

1. Uke grabs nage´s both wrists. Tenchi nage means heaven and earth throw. This is a refrence to that one hand goes upwards (heaven),and the other hand goes downwards (earth) while entering.

2. Nage takes a step 45 degrees off the attacking line into a stance cutting across the attacking line. One hand goes up towards the chin, while the other hand stretches out to the side and behind uke.

3. Nage turn hip and body and enters with a step close to uke.

4. Nage finishes the throw in a strong and well balanced position.

SHOMEN UCHI IRIMI NAGE

1. Nage initiates the technique by executing a shomen uchi and uke mimics the motion.

2. Nage enters into the back of uke while preparing to grab the lapel.

3. Nage enters while turning hip and body 180 degrees. It is important to stand not too close to uke. If uke is too close, the next movement will prove to be difficult and there will simply not be enough space between nage and uke to perform the breaking of the balance.

4. Nage lowers the center while pressing the hand holding the lapel to the chest. This tight contact is vital for the throw, since nage basically throws with the contact of the body. Nage still maintains the arm stretched out in order to control uke's arm.

SHOMEN UCHI IRIMI NAGE

5   Nage starts to turn hip and body another 180 degree turn while raising the arm.

6   Nage keeps turning until uke falls.

7   When uke starts to fall, nage's hip-turn is almost complete and nage takes the next step in close to uke.

8   Nage throws uke to the mat and afterwards stands in a good strong position.

GYAKI HANMI KATATE DORI KAITEN NAGE SOTO MAWARE

Nage will enter the technique on the outside of uke's arm, soto maware.

1. Uke grabs nage's wrist. Uke and nage start out in gyaki hanmi.

2. Nage steps 90 degrees off the attacking line into horse stance, breaks the balance and executes an atemi.

3. Nage forcefully turns the hip and executes an atemi with tegatana towards uke's face.

4. Nage steps in as a part of the atemi movement. Uke will resist the attack and strongly pushes back the hand.

GYAKI HANMI KATATE DORI KAITEN NAGE SOTO MAWARE

5 Nage leads uke's arm downwards, causing uke to lose balance.

6 Nage places one hand at the edge of the crown of the head, pushing uke down and backwards.
The placement of the hand on uke's head is vital. If placed on top of the head or close to the neck, uke will still have a lot of strength to resist. However if nage places the hand just where the top of the head turns into the neck of the head and applies pressure in a circular movement, uke will not be able to resist.

7 Nage turns hip and body to align with uke's direction in a 90 degree turn, simultaneously slides backwards and raises the arm and pushing the arm.
With the movement in pictures 6 and 7, nage forces uke's head down and backwards. Note that nage does not raise the arm until uke is properly pushed down and backwards.

8 Nage ends the technique in a strong and balanced position.

GYAKI HANMI KATATE DORI KAITEN NAGE UCHI MAWARE

Nage will enter the technique on the inside of uke's arm, uchi maware.

1. Uke grabs nage's wrist. Uke and nage start out in gyaki hanmi.

2. Nage steps 90 degrees off the attacking line, breaks the balance and executes an atemi.

3. Nage raises the hand and steps in under the arm.

4. Nage turns body and hip and strikes an atemi towards uke's face. This is a strong forceful movement.

GYAKI HANMI KATATE DORI KAITEN NAGE UCHI MAWARE

5 In order for uke not to be struck, uke will push back using the force needed. Nage completes the movement and ends up toe to toe, 45 degrees off the attacking line.

6 As uke pushes back the tegetana, nage leads uke's force downwards causing uke to lose balance.

7 At the lowest point, nage places one hand at the edge of the crown of uke's head. Nage fixates the head's position and keeps the head at this level for the remainder of the technique.

8 Nage raises the arm and slides backwards.

GYAKI HANMI KATATE DORI KAITEN NAGE UCHI MAWARE

9 Nage maintains the pressure at the head while pushing the arm diagonally across the center of uke. At this point uke should already be on the verge of falling over his own center.

2 Nage turns hip and body and uke falls forward.

3 Nage ends the technique in a strong and balanced postion.

4 Detail. Important technical notes for kaiten nage. Place the hand on the edge of the crown of the head. If you place the hand either on top of the head or the neck, uke will be strong and may easily stand up. Always maintain the pressure for that reason.
The arm should be pushed diagonally across uke's center towards the neck for maximum effect.

1ST SUBURI

1st Suburi - Ichi no Suburi

The first suburi is the base for the rest of the suburis with bokken. You can see many similarities with this first movement all the way through in the aikido curriculum in regards to the hip movement, stance and posture. For instance tai no henko, ikkyo, irimi nage and most other situations. So by practising bukiwaza you will also strengthen the tai jutsu side of aikido. Saito Sensei used to refer to O Sensei saying, when practising tai jutsu have the feeling of buki waza, and when practising buki waza have the feeling of tai jutsu.

1   You start out in ken kamae. You hold the bokken in a relaxed manner. The end of the bokken should point approximately at your belly button. The tip, when starting out, should point slightly upwards. When in partner practice the tip should basically be the only thing your partner should see. In practise however you end with the bokken horisontally.

2-3 Raise the sword straight up in a direct line with the center. The movement starts with a hip movement, iniating all other movement in the strike. The hip turn causes the front foot to slide slightly backwards.

4   You raise the bokken all the way up and to your back.

1ST SUBURI

5 When initiating the descent of the strike, you start with a hip movement and slide slightly forward with the front foot.

6-7 The strike comes down in the direct center. You center all motion in to your own center, pulling the elbows into a more narrow position.

8 The strike ends in the same position relative to your body as it started. This is important since it makes it possible for continous attacks and defences without corrections of your position.

1ST SUBURI

1st Suburi - Ichi no Suburi

1. Start out in hanmi and hold bokken in your center. The end pointing approximately to the belly button.

2. Raise the bokken straight up. The movement is initiated from the hip. Synchronize yor breathing with the movement. Inhale through your nose when raising the bokken and exhale through your mouth when letting the strike fall. You actually find strength in exhaling, and using your abdomen to pressure out the air from your lungs. The movement should be one. One continous movement, inhaling and exhaling, raising and striking.

3. Let the bokken move all the way back in basic practise. In partner pratcise this is not necessary or even generally advisable, since the movement in partner practise is genrally a smaller movement.

4. When moving in for the strike you turn the hip and the hip movement pulls out the bokken's movement.

1ST SUBURI

5. You strike with the exact same movement as when striking shomen uchi.

6. You end the strike horisontally. The position should be without correction leaving you ready for continous movement.

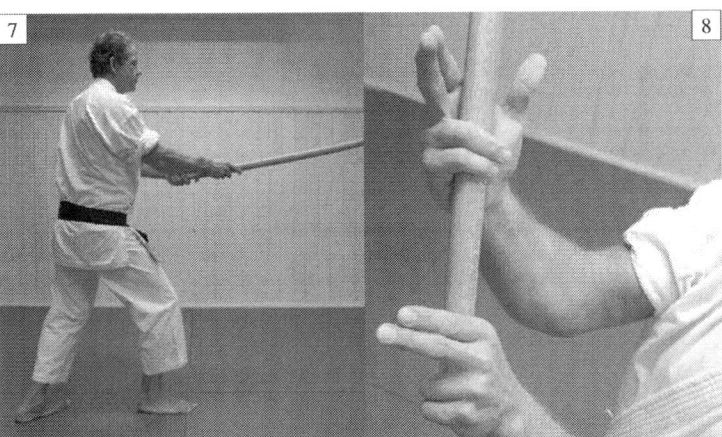
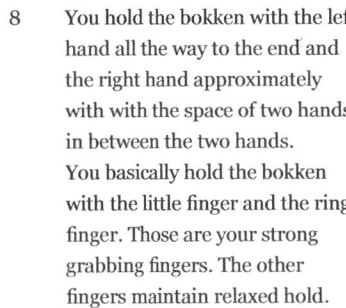
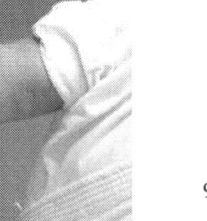
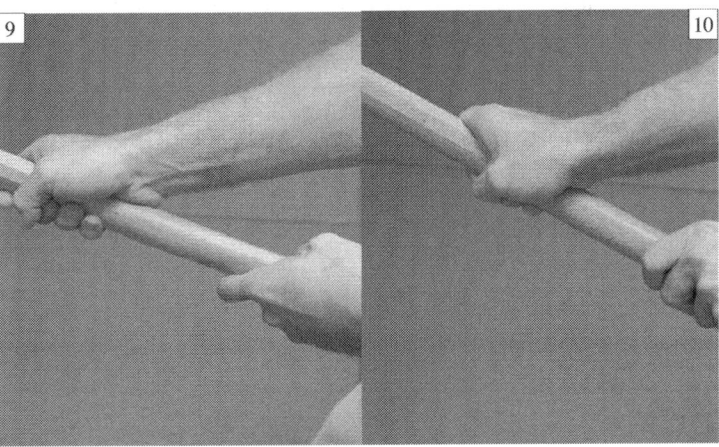

7. You hold the bokken in the center with the end pointing to your center and about the height of the belly button.

8. You hold the bokken with the left hand all the way to the end and the right hand approximately with with the space of two hands in between the two hands. You basically hold the bokken with the little finger and the ring finger. Those are your strong grabbing fingers. The other fingers maintain relaxed hold.

9. The hold when not actually striking is relaxed and therefore sensitive to any contact and pressure.

10. When ending a strike you turn your wrists inwards with the feeling of wringing out a wet rag. Note that you only turn the wrists, not all the way up and including your elbows. At this point the grip with the little fingers and ring fingers grab strongly, but also you let the inside of the index finger's joints lock on top of the bokken. This ensures that all kokyu power is extended through the bokken.

2ND SUBURI

2nd Suburi - Ni no Suburi
The 2nd suburi is a movement where you move out of the way of an attack, then swiftly being able to move back in on the attacking line to strike.

1. Start out in the same position as in 1st suburi.

2. Raise the bokken, turn the hip off the attacking line, maintain hanmi and keep the bokken aligned with the attacking line. Lower the hip and keep a balanced position with equal balance on both feet. You are supposed to be able to move with power and speed, therefore you need to have a lowered position in contradiction to standing with straight legs.

3. Turn your hip to re-enter the attacking line, drop the bokken to your back.

4. Continue to turn the hip and thereby take a step in.

2ND SUBURI

5   With both feet firm on the ground, continue to let the hip drive the strike down.

6   End the strike in the same manner as in 1st suburi.

2nd Suburi - Ni no Suburi

1   Start out in ken kamae.

2   Turn the hip and raise the sword.

2ND SUBURI

3   Turn hip and body off the attacking line. Raise the sword straight above the head. When holding the sword straight above the head it will move with your center and easily will follow any change of direction you decide to take.

4   Enter in to the low stance from where you can gather the base for a strong movement.

5   Turn the hip to re-enter on the attacking line.

6   When turning hip and body, eventually the step will follow.

2ND SUBURI

7 When in place you let the strike fall.

8 End the strike swith the bokken horisontally.

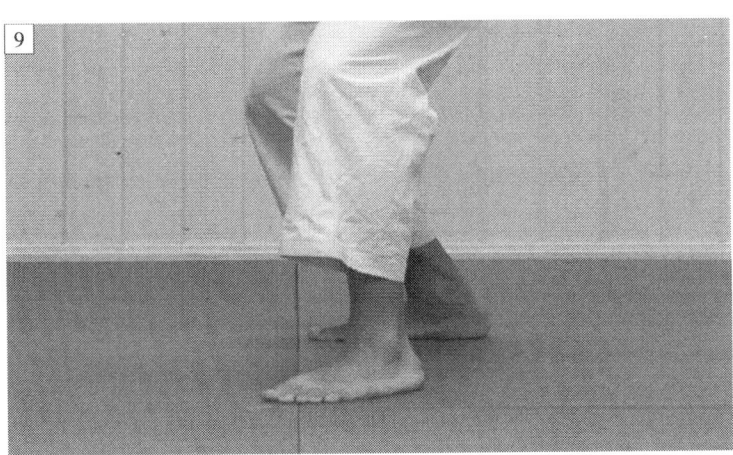

9 Turn the hip and body off the attacking line. The hip turn will decide how much off the attacking line you end up. However you only need to get off the line and not transport yourself a long distance. If you move too much off the line, you will not be able to reach your partner in the consecutive movements.

3RD SUBURI

3rd Suburi - San no Suburi
The 3rd suburi is a practice of a strong strike when moving forward with a big step or leap.

1 Start out in ken kamae.

2 Initiate the movement by turning the hip, and raise the bokken.

3 When turning the hip and raising the sword, take a step off the attacking line.

4 Move off the attacking line into horse stance. Let the bokken remain on the attacking line all the way through the suburi. The edge of the blade should at all times point forward and/or upwards.

3RD SUBURI

5   Raise the bokken above your head.

6-7 Let the bokken merely rest in the hands and move freely when lowering your hands. In this way the bokken will maintain in the correct position.

8   Enter a low position with the bokken in front of the center.

3RD SUBURI

9-10 Turn hip and body and re-enter the attacking line. In the same motion raise the bokken above the head.

11 Take a step forward slightly off the attacking line.

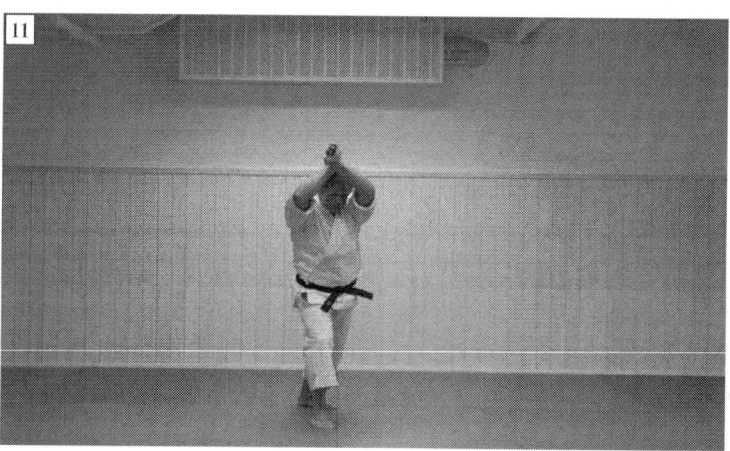

12-14 Let the strike fall when you are in place with both feet well grounded.

3RD SUBURI

14 End the strike with the bokken horisontally.

3rd Suburi - San no Suburi

1   Start out in ken kamae.

2   Turn hip and body and raise the sword.

3RD SUBURI

3   Raise the bokken above the head.

4   Turn the hip and body off the attacking line, and lower the bokken with the edge of the blade pointing forward. The bokken should be aligned with the attacking line from the beginning to the end of the suburi.

5   Hold the bokken in front the center with the edge of the bokken pointing upwards. The grasp of the bokken is very light all through the suburi until the end of the strike. The light hold is necessary for allowing the bokken to move freely in the hands.

6   Turn the hip and advance forward with a very big movement.

Saito Sensei used to say the feeling should be as if holding on to a rope, tied to a large rock that you would pull forward in one big movement.

3RD SUBURI

7-8 Turn the hip and advance in a big movement and then let the hip push the foot forward into a step forward.

9 Strike down when in balance and well grounded.

10 The strike ends with the bokken held horisontally.

4TH SUBURI

4th Suburi - Yon no Suburi
The 4th suburi is a series of consecutive strikes on the attacking line. You move along the attacking line and turn to move back.

1. Start out in ken kamae. 4th suburi starts out by executing the 2nd suburi.

2-3. Raise the bokken, turn hip and body off the attacking line and enter a low position.

4. Turn hip and body back on the attacking line and let the bokken drop all the way back.

4TH SUBURI

5-7   Take one step forward and strike down.

8-9   Turn the hip and move forward with a step, at the same time raise the bokken in your center.

4TH SUBURI

10 Strike down with the left foot forward, and left shoulder protruding while maintaining the same hold of the bokken.
Since you always hold the bokken with a right hand grip, in this instance you need to let the left shoulder protrude so that you can let the hip and stance maintain correct.

11-12 Turn the hip and take a step on to the attacking line while raising the bokken. Once taken the full step, strike with the bokken.

4TH SUBURI

13-15 Raise the sword and move forward one step. Strike down with the left foot forward, and left shoulder protruding while maintaining the same hold of the bokken.

Since you always hold the bokken with a right hand grip, in this instance you need to let the left shoulder protrude so that you can let the hip and stance maintain correct.

16 After several repititions of both right hand and left hand strikes, a common number is about 4, you make a change of direction. First turn the head to look in the direction you will take, 180 degree turn.

4TH SUBURI

17-18 After the turn of the head, turn hip and body and start raising the sword straight up above your head.

19-20 Strike straight down and continue with left hand and right hand strikes, until you turn again to finish with a strike in right hanmi.

5TH SUBURI

5th Suburi - Go no Suburi
The first 4 suburis are straight strikes aligned with the attacking line. Starting with the 5th suburi the strikes are slightly off the attacking line, coming in diagonally from the side. In taijutsu referred to yokomen uchi.
It is common to start out the 5th suburi first with the 2nd suburi. But it is also common to start out directly with yokomen uchi as here.

1. Start out in ken kamae.

2. Raise the bokken straight up from it's position and step off the attacking line directly under the bokken. It is important that you do not raise the bokken while pulling it backwards. You want to maintain the tip off the bokken pointing forward and not loose it's place. When raising the bokken, you basically just raise your hands in one synchronized movement, while stepping forward to move in under your hands.

3. Turn hip and body around. The hip movement will make your foot and bokken follow into place.

4-5. Strike down. When striking slowly your strike will almost be straight down but coming from the side off the attacking line. When striking with great speed and power, the movement will inevitably cause the bokken to come even more from the side. However your goal is to use your hip movement to turn and strike, and strike with as much control as possible. Therefore you want the bokken to stay as much as possible in your own center and not swing out of the center like for instance a base ball bat.

5TH SUBURI

6-7   Raise the bokken in the same manner as before. Though in this stance it may prove difficult to maintain the full hold of the bokken, therefor maintain as much contact as possible so that you quickly can get the full hold back later on.
Turn the hip and let the foot follow and so will the bokken.

8-9   Strike as before, off the attacking line but towards a point on the attacking line.

5TH SUBURI

10 Raise the the bokken and step in under it.

11-13 Strike down with the left foot forward.

5TH SUBURI

14-15 Compare the turn to the turn made in 4 th suburi. You will find it is the same type of turn. First turn the head, then hip and body while rasing the sword.

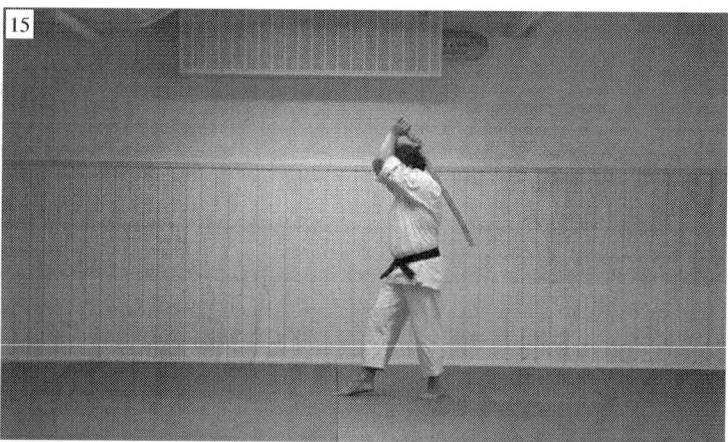

16-17 Strike down, as previous strikes, off the attacking line but aiming for a point on the attacking line.

5TH SUBURI

5th Suburi - Go no Suburi

1. Start out in ken kamae. When executing the 5th suburi, you will let bokken move across your most forward shoulder.

2. Raise the sword straight up, hands in the center while stepping slightly off the attacking line. You look between your hands and not over your shoulder.
Since you are moving forward while raising the bokken, it means you maintain control of the space in front of you rather than letting the bokken move backwards which would let an opponent take control of that same space. Executed correctly the bokken will also serve as protection when advancing.

3. Turn the hip and bring the foot in alignment with the hanmi, the bokken will just move round the center of your head into place.

5TH SUBURI

4-5 Initiate the strike from the hip and strike down.

6 Turn hip and body, step forward while raising the bokken in front of you.

7 Complete the body movement and be prepared to let the strike fall.

5TH SUBURI

8-9 Strike off the attacking line on to a point on the attacking line where your imaginary partner would stand.

6TH SUBURI

6th Suburi - Roku no Suburi
The 6th suburi is a combination of yokomen uchi and tsuki on the same side of the strike.

1-4 Start out in ken kamae, and perform the 2nd suburi.

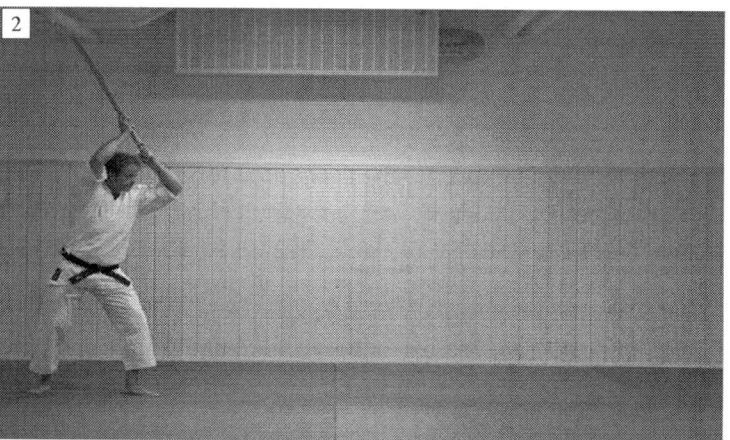

6TH SUBURI

5-6   Your thrust from the position where the strikes ends, meaning you do not pull back the bokken in order to advance with the thrust. There is no see-saw motion but a clean cut and then directly there after, thrust.

7-11   Turn the hip, step off the attacking line below the bokken and strike towards a point on the attacking line.

6TH SUBURI

11-13 Starting from where the strike finishes, you go directly in to the tsuki by pushing forward with hip and body. You turn the wrists so that the edge off the blade slightly points away from you, to the outside of your self.

6TH SUBURI

14-16 Start the turn by first turning the face in the next direction, 180 degree turn. Turn the hip and raise the bokken above the head and strike along the attacking line.

6TH SUBURI & 7TH SUBURI

17   Detail. Turn the wrists when executing the tsuki. The edge of the bokken should point away from your body.

7th Suburi - Shichi no Suburi
The 7th suburi is a combination of yokomen uchi and tsuki on the opposite side of the strike.

1-6   Start out in ken kamae and first perform the 2nd suburi.

7TH SUBURI

7-8 After the strike, turn the hip off the attacking line and step forward.

7TH SUBURI

9-11 Turn hip and body off the attacking line and raise the bokken and strike on to a point on the attacking line.

12-13 Turn the hip off the attacking line and perform a tsuki onto a point on the attacking lline.

7TH SUBURI

14-16 Turn hip and body 180 degree and strike along the attacking line.

SHIHO GIRI

Four directional cuts - Shiho giri

Shiho giri is a practice to strike in four different directions. The exercise is based on precise hip-movement and footwork.
There are several variations on how to perform shi ho giri.

1-4 Start out in ken kamae. Strike straight forward just like in the first suburi.

SHIHO GIRI

5-7 Turn 180 degrees by first turning head, hip and feet last. Raise the bokken above the head and simultaneously raise the bokken and strike straight along the line.

8-10 Turn 270 degrees by first turning head, hip and then feet, simultaneously raise the bokken and strike straight along the line.

SHIHO GIRI

11-13 Turn 180 degrees by first turning head, hip and feet last. Raise the bokken above the head and simultanousely raise the bokken and strike straight along the line.

SHIHO GIRI

14-15 Turn 90 degrees by first turning head, hip and feet last. Raise the bokken above the head and simultaneously raise the bokken and strike straight along the line.

15 The strikes are executed in this order, first straight, then with a left turn, then a right turn until finished in the following angles.
0
180
270
180
90

HAPPO GIRI

Eight directional cuts - Happo giri

Happo giri is a practice to strike in eight different direction with the correct hip movement and foot work.

1-3 Start out in ken kamae and strike straight forward just like in the first suburi.

4-5 Turn hip and body 180 degrees and strike straight along the attacking line.

HAPPO GIRI

6-8 Turn head first then hip and body 270 degrees, simultaneously raise the bokken. and strike straight along the attacking line.

HAPPO GIRI

9-11 Turn 180 degrees and strike along the line.

12-14 Turn 225 degrees and cut straight forward.

HAPPO GIRI

15-16 Turn 180 degrees and strike straight forward.

HAPPO GIRI

17-19 Turn hip and body 270 degrees and strike straight.

20-22 Turn 180 degrees and strike straight.

HAPPO GIRI

23-27 Turn 315 degrees, seven eighths of a full circle and strike straight.

HAPPO GIRI

27 The strikes are executed in this order, first straight, the with a left turn, then a right turn untill finished in the following angles.
0
180
270
180
225
245
180
270
180
315 (7/8)

Tanren uchi is a necessary practice to develop powerful strikes and strong and stable hip movements. I strongly recommend building your own tanren for this purpose. It is also wise to consult someone who knows how to practise with tanren or else you may end up creating bad habits in your training.

Jo Suburi

The Jo suburis are divided into several segments. First there are five thrusting movements. Then there are five striking movements. This followed by three one-handed wrist movements. The fourth segment is five so called figure eight movements. This is a reference to the japanese character for the number 8, 八. When writing the japanese character yo would first draw the left line, starting from the top, then the second line, to the right, also starting from the top. This is pretty much the way you also execute a hasso technique. Finally the last segment are the two flowing forms, that commonly are also put together into one flowing form.

Tsuki no Bu
1 - Choku Tsuki
2 - Kaeshi Tsuki
3 - Ushiro Tsuki
4 - Tsuki Gedan Gaeshi
5 - Tsuki Jodan Gaeshi

Uchi Komi no Bu
6 - Shomen Uchi Komi
7 - Renzoku Uchi Komi
8 - Men Uchi Gedan Gaeshi
9 - Men Uchi Ushiro Tsuki
10 - Gyaku Yokomen Ushiro Tsuki

Not included in the beginners guide.

Katate no Bu
11 - Katate Gedan Gaeshi Uchi
12 - Katate Toma Uchi
13 - Katate Hachi no Ji Gaeshi

Hasso Gaeshi no Bu
14 - Hasso Gaeshi Uchi
15 - Hasso Gaeshi Tsuki
16 - Hasso Gaeshi Ushiro Tsuki
17 - Hasso Gaeshi Ushiro Uchi
18 - Hasso Gaeshi Ushiro Barai/harai

Nagare no Bu
19 - Hidari Nagare Gaeshi Uchi
20 - Migi Nagare Gaeshi Tsuki

Grip

When holding the jo or the bokken for that matter, it is important not to clench but to hold gently. This way lets you easily move the weapon effortlessly. Holding gently is a general recommendation until the moment when you finalize a technique in a strike or thrust. Then at the end you should turn the wrists to lock onto the weapon and obtain a firm hold that will enable you to harness the impact of the attack. The knuckles of the index fingers ends up on top off the weapon, while you grasp strongly with the little fingers as well as the ring fingers.

Positioning and stance

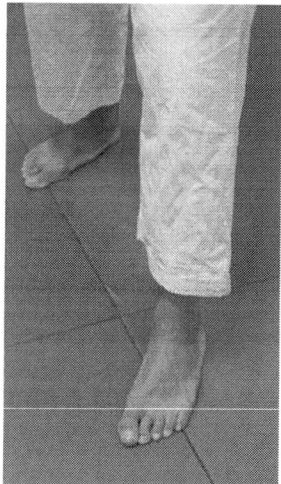

When in jo kamae, start out with the end pointing slightly upwards, The idea is to have the end to be basically the only part of the jo visible to any partner. The angle should therefore vary depending on the partners height.

The stance should be, when in jo kamae, similar to the ordinary stance called hanmi. However when working with jo you stand with the front foot slightly off the line. Always stand straight, with both legs slightly bent and with a centered feeling in your body. Your head should be erect aligning with your spine.

 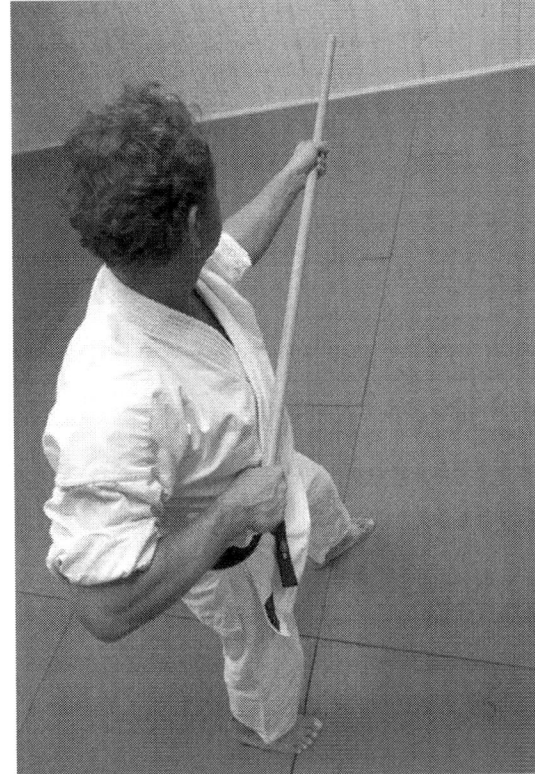

The jo is held close to the body.

Jo kamae. The starting position in jo. The tip of the jo is pointing up to a point where the opponent only can see the very tip of the jo. The angle of the jo naturally will vary depending on the distance between the two practitioners.

CHOKU TSUKI

Choku Tsuki

1. Start in Jo kamae.

2. Lift the jo by holding it by the center. Lift the jo with both hands. At the same time slide forward slightly off the attacking line.

3. Let the right hand slide down to the end of the jo as you in that movement pull the jo down into a horisontal level. The left hand slides simultaneously forward.

4. Strike the tsuki and lock the grip of the jo tightly by turning the wrists.

KAESHI TSUKI

Kaeshi Tsuki

1   Start out in Jo kamae.

2-5   Grab hold of the jo from above. Pull the jo straight up and move off the line into kamae and lay the jo in a horisontal position.

KAESHI TSUKI & USHIRO TSUKI

6   End with a horisontal tsuki.

Ushiro Tsuki

1   Start out in kamae.
    There is a number of variations on how you can practise. I prefer to make a distinct hip turn and maintain the head facing forward all the way through. Once the suburi is finished you can check your progress but do not let your eyes lead your aim. It is also possible to end with various degrees of hip turns, 180 and 90 degrees where you often end in horse stance.

2   Hold the jo by the center and lift it straight up, at the same time grab the top end of the jo. Let the jo align tightly to the forearm. By using the forearm you will aim the jo in a straight line to it's target, and from there being able to thrust straight.

USHIRO TSUKI

5 Turn the hip and lift the jo and at the same time start aiming by tilting the elbow in the correct angle. In the basic form you aim for the imaginary partner's knee.

6 Once the hip can turn no further, take a step back and maintain the aim.

7 Using the whole hip turn from the start you will have the energy and power for the thrust.

TSUKI GEDAN GAESHI

Tsuki gedan gaeshi

1 - Start out in tsuki no kamae.

2   Move forward, slightly off the line. When moving maintain the jo in it's position so that you do not pull the jo back and open up for your partner to enter in your space. Once off the attacking line and in kamae, strike a tsuki.

3-4   Turn the hip and let one foot cross the line, with the same hip turn pull back the jo into gedan gaeshi position.

TSUKI GEDAN GAESHI

5-7   Turn the hip and step forward still 45 degrees off the attacking line. With this movement you start a strike towards an opponents front knee. The movement should go upwards in an arch and then down at the height of a knee.

You keep your hands at the height of your own chest all through the strike. The strike resembles in many ways a yokomen uchi, even though the hold of the jo is different.

TSUKI JODAN GAESHI

Tsuki Jodan Gaeshi

1   Start out in tsuki no kamae.

2   Move forward off the attacking line and strike a tsuki.

3-4   Turn the hip and step across the attacking line. Move both hands to the center of the jo and prepare to lift it above the head. With the hip turn move into hanmi.

114

TSUKI JODAN GAESHI

5   Turn the jo around above the head and let the left hand slide along the jo to grip at the end.

6-8   Step forward still slightly off the attacking line and strike a shomen uchi.

SHOMEN UCHI KOMI

Shomen Uchi Komi

1. Start out in ken no kamae. This exercise is identical to the ni no suburi, bokken.

2. Turn the hip backwards, step backwards off the line while lifting the jo above the head. Maintain the jo aligned with the attacking line.

3. Turn the hip and step back on the attacking line. In basic form practise it is common to drop the jo all the way back to gain a larger and more relaxed form. In partner practice you would not drop the jo all the way down but maintain the high posture of (2) and strike directly down.

4. Strike a shomen uchi.

RENZOKU UCHI KOMI

Renzoku Uchi Komi

This is a combined exercise of the shomen uchi komi and a yokomen uchi.

1-4 Start out in ken no kamae, then take a step back slightly off the attacking line. Let the jo remain on the attacking line. Turn hip and body back onto the attacking line and strike a shomen uchi.

RENZOKU UCHI KOMI

5-7 Step forward, slightly off the attacking line and execute a yokomen uchi.

MEN UCHI GEDAN GAESHI

Men Uchi Gedan Gaeshi

1-3 Start out in ken no kamae, then take a step back slightly off the attacking line. Let the jo remain on the attacking line. Turn hip and body back onto the attacking line and strike a shomen uchi.

4 Slide off the attacking line to the left, simultaneously pull the jo back and conceal the jo behind your body.

MEN UCHI GEDAN GAESHI

5-7 Turn the hip and step forward slightly off the attacking line, at the same time start raising the jo in an arch-like movement. The aim is to strike from above and the side across an imaginary opponent's knee.

8 Detail. Strike towards the knee and stay off the attacking line.

9 Detail. Conceal the jo behind your body. As in picture no. 4.

MEN UCHI USHIRO TSUKI

Men Uchi Ushiro Tsuki

1-4 Perform shomen uchi komi. Start out in ken kamae, then take a step back slightly off the attacking line. Let the jo remain on the attacking line. Turn hip and body back onto the attacking line and strike a shomen uchi.

MEN UCHI USHIRO TSUKI

5. Turn the hip and move off the attacking line to the left and into hanmi. With your left hand, pull the jo straight back, simultaneously turn the hip in the same direction, when doing this let your right hand slide forward to the front end of the jo.

6. Aim for a point on the attacking line and with a single strong hip turn strike the tsuki in chest height.

GYAKU YOKOMEN USHIRO TSUKI

Gyaku Yokomen Ushiro Tsuki

1-4 Move straight into yokomen uchi and there by end up slightly off the attacking line to the left.

GYAKU YOKOMEN USHIRO TSUKI

5   Using your left hand, pull the jo in the same direction you are turning the hip, to the right. Connect the jo to your forearm and let the fore am guide the jo in it's aim. Aim for a horisontal thrust at chest height.
You are going to make a 180 degree turn. Step off the attacking line with your right foot.

6   Grab the back end of the jo with your left hand.

7-8 Continue the hip turn and the tsuki. Step slightly off the attacking line with both feet and aim, in an angle, at an opponent on the attacking line.

WORD LIST FOR AIKIDOKAS

Agatsu	"Self victory."
Aikido	The word is made up from three different characters. Ai meaning harmony, Ki meaning spirit or universal energy and DO maning the way/path.
Aiki doka	Aikido practioner
Aiki kai	Means aikido association and commonly refers to the organization of the Ueshiba family.
Ai uchi	Means mutual kill, a term to describe the outcome of an encounter were both participants are killed.
Atemi	Means striking the body. An atemi is a blow to the opponent used for unbalancing and distracting the opponent. The blow may be fierce or not depending on the situation at hand. O Sensei and Saito Sensei used to say that Aikido is 99% atemi underlining the importance of atemi in aikido practice. In Iwama there were also tools for atemi training such as the makiwara.
Baka	Fool/idiot.
Barai	Also harai. To parry or ward off.
Bokken	Also refered to as bokuto. The bokken is a sword made out of wood, most commonly japanese white oak.
Budo	Often translated as martial art or martial way/path.
Buki waza	Weapons practice
Choku tsuki	Direct straight tsuki
Chudan	Means middle position.
Dai	Great/big compare with O, as in O-Sensei.
Daito ryu aikijutsu	A school headed by Sokaku Takeda which heavily influenced the development of aikido.
Dan	Dan is a black belt rank.
Dame	Wrong/bad
Deshi	Student
Do	The way/path
Do In	Traditoin of self massage often in connection with training
Dojo	Means a place for practice, a place for the path.
Dojo cho	The head of a dojo
Domo arigato gozai mashita	A very polite way of saying thank you.
Doshu	The Head of the path, The head of Aikikai
Eri	Neck, lapel
Eri dori	Grab of the lapel by the neck.
Furi kaburi	To raise the sword above the head.
Futari dori	Training with two attackers
Gaeshi	Also Kaeshi, reversed/turning.
Ganseki otoshi	Throwing technique where nage lifts uke above the head and shoulders and drops uke like a rock straight down.
Gasshuku	Training camp
Gedan	Lower position
Geri	Kick
Gi	keiko gi, do gi refers to the clothes worn in aikido practice. Most common in Iwama style dojos is the Karate gi.
Gokyo	The fifth technique, pinning technique. Designed especially for knife taking situations.
Gomen nasai	Exscuse me, I am sorry.
Go tai	hard body, refers to a rigorous way of training. Used in the purest form of basic form training. Compare ju tai and ryu tai. The three forms are often used in conjunction as a progression in training, going from hard to completely flowing techniques in order to fully grasp the depth and width of techniques.
Gyaku yokomen	Reversed cut to the side of the head.
Hajime	Begin/start.
Hanmi	Used in Ai hanmi where uke and nage stands with the same foot forward and gyaki hanmi where uke and nage stands with opposing feet, left/right foot forward. It is a stance where the practitioner forms a triangular stance with the feet and creates as a small target as possible. This is also described as Hito Emi. A stance that origintaes from sword paractice
Hanmi handachi waza	A starting position where nage is sitting in seiza and uke is standing.
Happo giri	Eight directional cut used primarily in bokken practice.
Hasso no kamae	This stance refers to the japanese character for the number 8.

WORD LIST FOR AIKIDOKAS

Haya gaeshi	Quick turn
Henka waza	Technical variations. Compare to Ki hon waza which means basic techniques. Henka waza refers to the existing variations of a basic technique for instance ikkyo.
Hidari	Left
Hiji	Elbow
Hiji dori	Grab by the elbow
Hito Emi	See Hanmi
Ikkyo	The first technique, pinning technique.
Irimi	Means literary entering the body. Specifically used in Irimi nage.
Irimi nage	Entering throw
Jinja	The Aiki Shrine. Located in Iwama, Ibaraki prefecture, Japan.
Jiyu waza	Practice where ultimately there are no pre-decided tachniques nor attacks.
Jo	Staff made of wood, japanese white oak.
Jodan	Upper position.
Jo dori	Jo taking techniques
Jo kamae	Starting position with jo held vertically.
Jo nage	Techniques throwing uke with the jo.
Juji garamae	Cross twine throw
Ju tai	Soft body, refers to a smooth way of training. Compare go tai and ryu tai.
Kaeshi waza	Counter techniques
Kaiso	The founder of Aikido, Morihei Ueshiba.
Kamae	Stance
Kami	A spirit, divinity.
Kata	A predestined series of movements.
Kata dori	Grab by the shoulder
Katate dori	Grab by the wrist
Keiko	Training
Ken	Sword
Ken kamae	Starting position with bokken.
Ki	Spirit, energy, universal life force.
Kiai	A shout that focuses all energy in body and mind into one focused movement.
Kihon	Basic form in practice.
Ki musubi	Tying ki together.
Kaiten nage	Rotary throw
Kohai	Junior student
Kokoro	Heart/mind
Kokyu	Breathing
Kokyu ho	Breathing exercise/technique. Fundamental part of any technique in aikido. Manifested by the unification of breathing, mind, body into one.
Kokyu nage	A vast variation of throws using kokyu power. Originally Irimi nage was counted as a kokuyu nage.
Kosa	Cross over.
Kosa dori	Kosa dori, same grab as ai hanmi katate dori
Koshi nage	Hip throw
Kote geashi	Turning wrist throw
Kubi shime	Choke
Kuden	Oral tradition. Refers to orally conveyed nuggets of wisdom.
Kumi jo	Jo partner practice
Kumi tachi	Bokken partner practice
Kuzushi	It is a Japanese term for unbalancing uke in various aspects, as well physically as mentally.
Kyu	White belt rank
Ma ai	Harmonius distance. A distance between uke and nage where neither can reach the other.
Mai	Front/forward. Mai Ukemi, forward roll.
Makiwara	Makiwara is a padded striking post used as a training tool
Mudansha	Students without black belt ranks
Muna dori	Grab by the chest lapel
Mushin	Means, no mind. A state of genitive awareness.
Nagare	Flowing as in flowing techniques.
Nage	Person executing the technique, compare shite/tori.
Nikkyo	The second technique, pinning technique.
Obi	Belt
Omote	Means the front, as in the front of uke. It is used as a description of how a technique is performed, omote waza. Compare, ura waza.
Onegai shimasu	When initation practice, both practioners bow to each other and say Onegai shimasu. I welcome you to train with me (Please).
Osai waza	Pinning techniques
O-Sensei	Means Great teacher. Morihei Ueshiba, founder of aikido.
Oyo waza	Applied techniques.
Randori	In randori usually there is only one uke but in jyu waza there are several ukes. Free attacks and defences.
Reigi	Ettiquette
Rokyo	The sixth technique, pinning technique.

WORD LIST FOR AIKIDOKAS

Ryu tai	Flowing body, refers to a flowing way of training. Compare go tai and ju tai.
Ryo	As in grabbing with two hands on two places. Compare Ryote dori.
Ryote dori	Grab of both wrists
Sankyo	The third technique, pinning technique.
Sannin dori	Training with three attackers
Sensei	Teacher, means literary person born before you.
Seiza	Sitting on one´s knees.
Sempai	A student senior to oneself
Shihan	Means, a teacher of techers, master instructor.
Shi ho nage	Four directional throw.
Shikaki	A dead angle position where uke have difficulty seeing nage.
Shikko	Knee walking.
Shite	Also called nage and/or tori
Shodan	First degree black belt.
Shomen	Front or top of the head. Refers also to the centerpiece of the dojo.
Shomen uchi	Strike to the side of the head
Sode dori	Grab of the sleeve.
Sode guchi dori	Grab of the cuff of the sleeve.
Soto	Outside
Soto deshi	A student living outside the dojo area.
Suburi	Solitary basic form practice in bokken and jo.
Suwari waza	Techniques where both uke and nage are sitting down in seiza.
Tachi	Sword
Tachi waza	Training while standing
Tachi dori	Sword taking techniques
Tai jutsu	Body techniques, unarmed techniques.
Tai no henko	Basic training form where nage learns how to blend, control and enter close by uke. Tai no tankan is a term used for the same movement.
Tai sabaki	Body movement. Different exercises designed to enhanced the ability to move with stability.
Takemusu aiki	A concept where an aikidoka through mastery of the basic forms develop skills to infinitely generate techniques in the spur of the moment.
Taninsugake	Training with multiple attackers.
Tanren uchi	A training tools devised for forging a strong and stable hip movement along with a synchronized kokyu practice.
Tanto	A dagger.
Tanto dori	Knife taking techniques
Tegetana	Means hand sword. Refers to the edge of the hand.
Tenchi nage	Heaven and earth throw
Tenkan	Turning movement.
Tori	Nage compare also shite.
Tsuki	Thrust or astrike/punch.
Uchi	Inside.
Uchi	Cut
Uchi deshi	A student living inside the dojo area.
Uke	A person receiving the techniques.
Ukemi	Means, receiving with the body. Mae ukemi forward falls/rolls, ushiro ukemi backward falls/rolls.
Ura	Rear often in techniques on the outside of uke for instance, ikkyo ura waza,
Ushiro	Behind/rear.
Waza	Techniques.
Yame	Stop
Yoko	Side
Yokomen	Side of the head.
Yokomen uchi	Strike to the side of the head.
Yonkyo	The forth technique, pinning technique.
Yudansha	Person holding a black belt rank.
Zanshin	A prolonged focus. Maintaining the focus even after the completion of a technique.

Some examples of how you describe the techniques in class

Starting position	Form of attack	Technique	How the technique is performed	
Ai hanmi	Katate dori	Ikkyo	Omote waza	(Ki hon/Ki no nagagre)
Ai hanmi*	Shomen uchi	Shi ho nage	Ura waza	
Gyaki hanmi*	Katate dori*	Tai no henko	Go tai/ju tai/ryu tai/ki hon/ ki no nagare	
Ai hanmi'	Shomen uchi	Irimi nage	Kihon waza	
Gyaki hanmi	Kata dori	Nikkyo	Ura waza	
Hanmi handachi waza	Katate dori	Shiho nage	Omote waza	
Suwari waza	Ryote dori*	Kokyu ho		

*Usually not said or defined in class. Since the form in itself is obviously set in a predefined manner.

SOME ADVICE FOR NEW STUDENTS IN A DOJO

WHEN YOU ARE NEW IN A DOJO. HERE ARE SOME GOOD ADVICE.

In the dojo
When you as a student first enter a dojo there are a few things you should pay special attention to. Most dojos follow a certain reigi, etiquette, which is designed for the participants to enjoy mutual respect, a safe and beneficial learning environment. This is what you most likely will encounter and should adhere to;

Preparations
General good advice is to come in good time so you do not rush into class but rather have the time to settle down and calm your mind. Make sure you have eaten and had water.

Hygiene
Alllways be fresh and free of odor! Keep your finger and toe nails short. Your keiko gi should never be smelly or unsavory in any way. Before you enter the mat you must always wash your hands and feet.

Reigi
You bow towards the shomen before entering the mat and before leaving the mat. This is important since this tells you and your fellow aikidokas that you area prepared to practice.

You never enter the mat in case class is in action without obtaining the teachers attention and approval. This is important since the teacher must be aware of who is on the mat.

You never leave the mat without consulting the teacher first. This is important since your teacher is responsible for everybody's safety on or off the mat in the dojo. For instance, if a person is in any way injured he/she may sneak off the mat and pass out without anyone be the wiser. Unless he/she prior talked with the teacher this can turn out to be a dangerous situation.

Beginning of class
All students sit in a row in front of the shomen. This is looking at the group from behind. Facing the shomen, senior students, sempai, sit in order of the most senior student to the far right. The less senior students (kohai) sit to the far left. Initially all bow towards the shomen and clap their hands. Then the teacher turns to the students, bows and greet them with **Onegai shimasu**. The students bow with the teacher and say **Onegai Shimasu**. This basically means, I welcome you to train with me (Please).

This exact ritual is repeated at the end of class with the difference of the wording. At the end all say instead, **Domo Arigato Gozaimashita**. This means Thank you. (In a most polite form). These two phrases will be repeated on many occasions during class.

Every time after the teacher has shown a technique you find a partner, you both will bow, standing or sitting down, and say the correct corresponding phrase. This goes without saying that you do the same when ending a practice of technique when the teacher claps his/her hands. The importance of this is that you let your partner know that you are prepared and ready to train, or that you both have concluded practice.

SOME ADVICE FOR NEW STUDENTS IN A DOJO

During class
During class all pay attention to the teacher and what is said. During class the teacher will often give students personalized remarks on how to improve their technique and training. These are things said to encourage and help to develop a student. When this happens, the student receiving the comment will say **Domo Arigato Gozaimashita** and the other student/students nearby will say **Onegai Shimasu**, meaning they are also ready to learn more and receive comments.

Always train with a good humor and in a kind gentle spirit
Train with sincerity in every way. Remember if you are a sempai, the faster you help younger students evolve and grow, the faster you will have more skilled partners in the future. We are all kohai at some point, and also sempai as time goes by.

Try to avoid unnecessary talk in class since this will inevitably ruin the focus for you and your fellow practitioners. Traditionally you do not leave the mat for water. This is something you are supposed to have taken care prior to class. Once you are on the mat, all your focus belongs there.

If you would unintentionally arrive late or have to leave class early
If you for any good reason would arrive late wait for the instructor to acknowledge your presence and for the ok to enter the mat. Then you sit down at the edge of mat and perform the full starting bow, with claps and correct phrase. This should be done loud and clear so that everybody would know that another student is prepared to start practise. If you would have to leave class before it finishes, ask permission to leave class, then perform the same ritual as when finishing class. This too should be done loud and clear for the same above mentioned reason.

Outside of class
Common sense goes a long way. In a dojo you try to build a trusting and respectful atmosphere. Without this it is hard to train any martial art. Therefore all students need to think about paying attention to the culture within the dojo and treat fellow aikidokas the same way you expect to be treated. Be nice, helpful, attentative and sincere in your precense.

Made in the USA
Middletown, DE
27 October 2020